You and Your Pendulum

Carol Calmes
2nd Edition

Balboa Press books may be ordered through booksellers or by contacting:

Balboa Press
A Division of Hay House
1663 Liberty Drive
Bloomington, IN 47403
www.balboapress.com
1 (877) 407-4847

Bridge Illustration and Script copyrighted to Carol Calmes
Stock Images from Getty Images and Pixabay

ISBN: 978-1-9822-4175-9 (sc)
ISBN: 978-1-9822-4176-6 (e)

Library of Congress Control Number: 2020901174

Print information available on the last page.

Balboa Press rev. date: 03/03/2020

BALBOA.PRESS

Our Bridge

Our Connection

Our Awakening

Dedicated to:

My son, who was my inspiration to develop
"You and Your Pendulum"

Michael Joseph Calmes
March 30, 1989 to September 17, 2013

"You and Your Pendulum"

Step By Step Guided Tour On How To Use This Interactive Package

Our Bridge

Our Connection

Our Awakening

This Package Includes:

❖ Guided Tour – Getting To Know Your Pendulum

❖ Guided Step By Step To Getting Started

❖ Daily Use Chart

❖ Half Circle Chart Including A-Z & Seasons

❖ Half Circle Chart Including 1-31 & Seasons

❖ Six A-Z Guidance Sheets

❖ Who Are My Animal Spirit Guides

❖ Communicating With Your Furry Friends

❖ Three A-Z Create Your Own Guidance Sheets

❖ No Peeking Foldables

A GUIDED "STEP BY STEP" TOUR ON HOW TO USE THIS PACKAGE

First and foremost, thank you for choosing "You and Your Pendulum". Play, enjoy and have fun communicating thru this tool.

Many people believe that they are speaking with their higher self when they are using a pendulum. Are you really? It is very possible that your EGO is stepping in the way of your Higher Self and giving you answers/guidance that you want to hear. Then later-on you become disappointed because of what you asked or expected from your pendulum doesn't happen!

So here it is, a guide that will help you connect with your Higher Self, your Angelic team, Guides and Spirit of Loved Ones by following a few simple steps.

Choosing a pendulum that is right for you – At the time of purchase:
For this package it is suggested that your pendulum has a pointed end with some weight to it. The reasoning behind this is so that you can clearly see the direction or line that it is trying to give you a message on without any bulkiness impeding your view of the chart.

Choosing a pendulum that is right for you can be a very quick process or may take some time. Not only are you choosing it but it also is choosing you:

Hold your pendulum in your hand and cup both hands around it. Then say out loud with a strong and assertive intention "CLEAR". This should clear any energies that the pendulum may be holding onto from being handled by many people; for instance, manufacturing energy; being handled along its journey to the storefront and customers picking it up, trying it etc.

Programming Your Pendulum

Now hold your pendulum by placing your thumb and middle finger on the chain end (there may be a ball or flat end there) and allow the pendulum to hang quietly.

Many people have a different way that their pendulum would swing for yes or no; however, for this package ask (program) your pendulum to show you "YES" by swinging in a circle clockwise. Once you have established a strong swing in a clockwise direction then you will ask (program) your pendulum to show you "NO" by swinging back and forth straight out in front of you (it should swing inward towards your chest and outward away from your chest; not side to side).

Now that you've established the swing directions ask your pendulum "Are you meant for me?" If it says "yes" then ask again "Did you choose me?" If it says "yes" then ask "Should I buy you?" and one more question "Are you a good fit to work with this package" If it comes back yes, then that is the pendulum for you. If you receive a "NO" on any or all of these questions, then repeat the process with another Pendulum. You may find a number of pendulums that want to go home with you; so at that point you will have to make a choice on which one will suit you best for working with this package and to work with on a regular basis.

Further into this book you will find information on programming your pendulum to work with the charts provided.

Setting Your Sacred Space (Shielding Thoughts – Setting Intention)

In order to receive messages and guidance from your Higher Self, your Angelic team, Guides and Spirit of Loved Ones, it is important for you to "Set Your Sacred Space" in order to shield yourself from your own thoughts "EGO" and the thoughts of others. This way when you receive your message or your guidance you will know it is 100% Pure and is coming to you with Love & Light to serve you for your highest purpose and best interest.

The following is an intention that is recommended to be said before each session with this package (the shield will last for a day before needing to be repeated). You may reword the intention to what resonates with you. However, it is recommended that you please keep your intentions in 100% Pure Love & Light to get your best results.

Allowing yourself to "Trust" and have an open heart and mind with 100% pure intentions will give you greater results.

Throughout this book your Higher Self, Angelic team, Guides and Spirit of Loved Ones will be referred to as "Your Team".

Setting Your Sacred Space (Shielding Thoughts – Setting Intention)

Set and cup both your hands over the pendulum and say:

Archangel Michael, All Divine, All Of Which Who Belong With Me and Who Are Of 100% Pure White Light. I Now Set My Sacred Space. Please Shield Me To Prevent My Ego, Willful and Wishful Thinking And My Thoughts From Influencing Any Messages That I May Receive On My Pendulum.

Please Also Shield The Thoughts Of Others To Keep Them From Influencing Any Messages That I May Receive On My Pendulum.

Only Beings Of 100% Pure White Light, The Divine And Those Who Belong With Me Be Allowed To Communicate Loving, Truthful and Honest Messages Which Serve Me For My Highest Purpose And Which Are Only For My Best Interest.

I Am Aware That The Guidance I Receive Is For The "NOW" And The Messages I Receive Are The Messages I Will Accept. .... With Grace And Gratitude.

I Ask That I Am Always Shielded and Safe In Your White Light Of Protection Forever and Always.

So It Is. So It Is Set. So It Will be.

Test Your Pendulum - Programing your pendulum for "Daily Use Chart"

Hold your pendulum using your dominant hand and place your thumb and middle finger on the ball/handle at the end of the chain and place your non-dominant hand about 1" - 2" below the pendulum. With your mind ask your pendulum to show you "yes" and to show you "no".

The pendulum should hang completely still. It may have a slight vibration but it shouldn't move. What you have just done is shield your mind/thoughts from causing the pendulum to move.

Now you are ready to program your pendulum to work with your "Daily Use Chart"

Next: Ask a member from "Your Team" if they could please show you "YES" by swinging in a clockwise motion and that your "NO" swings back and forth from your chest outward. Next: Establish with "Your Team" when swinging counter clockwise it will represent "You are on the right path" "You are on the right track". The next step is establishing with "Your Team" when swinging diagonally outward to the right it would represent "Everything is going to be ok" or if you ask "How are you today?" it would represent "They are ok or doing great". The next step is establishing with "Your Team" when it swings diagonally outward to the left it would be a message to you that "You are Loved" or "I Love You".

When closing off your session always show Gratitude and say "Thank You".

Establish with "Your Team" that when you show Gratitude by saying "Thank You", that the pendulum swings side to side which represents "You're Welcome / Thank You" This type of programming establishes that it is not you creating the movement and that "Your Team" understands the directions you would like the swings of your pendulum to go in order to establish clear communication.

Now You Are Ready To Use Your Pendulum

Once you have completed the previous steps, you can start asking alternate questions, perhaps, "Is There A Message For Me Today?" "What Guidance Do You Have For Me Today?"

Personally, I prefer to know whom from my "Team" I am speaking with; so if the answer is "yes" then proceed to ask "Who is the message from?"

There is a wide range of possible Spiritual / Celestial Beings that you may be communicating with. For example, I would slowly list them off until I receive a "yes" for example:

Spirit Guides

If it comes back no; then go on to the next on this list and so on.

If it comes back "yes" and you know the name of your guides then you can start listing them off until it comes back "yes" again. If you don't know the names of your guides; then this would be a great opportunity to become introduced and asking what their names are, how many you have and allowing them to spell out their name for you on the chart. Then start communicating either thru the guidance sheets provided or allow them to spell out their message to you.

A Passed Loved One

It is beautiful when a passed one comes thru and wants to communicate. If you have several passed loved ones follow the same steps in naming them until you receive a "yes". Then start communicating either thru the guidance sheets provided or allow them to spell out their message to you.

Guardian Angel

We all were born with at least one guardian angel. Would you like to know his/ her name? Would you like to know if you have more than one? This would be a great opportunity to become acquainted and asking what their names are, how many you have and allowing them to spell out their name for you on the chart. Then start communicating either through the guidance sheets provided or allow them to spell out their message to you.

Archangels

There are many Archangels who would love to step in and help us in all aspects of our lives through guidance, signs & symbols; all you need to do is give them permission to step in and help you – Just Ask! If you get a "yes" that you have a message from one of these beautiful beings, then you can start listing off their names as we know them until you receive a "yes": The list below names some of the Archangels and their specialties. When permitted to do so, all Archangels have the power to help in every way but they also have a special skill of their own.

Michael - Protection, courage, money matters; **Raphael** - Healing, guidance, calm
Gabriel - Communication, creativity, speaking your truth; **Ariel** - Courage for change
Uriel - Life Lessons; **Sandalphon** - Prayer delivery and receiving blessings
Metatron - Aura cleansing; **Azrael** - Comfort for the dying, moving thru grief
Zadkiel - Emotional healing and forgiveness; **Jophiel** - Helps you focus in the now
Jeremiel - Life review, dreams, astral travel guide; **Haniel** -Third Eye clearing, accepting cycles of change
Chamuel - Attracting your vibrational match; **Raziel** -Past life understanding and healing; **Raguel** - Resolving situations, bringing balance

Higher Self / Spirit / Universe - Self Explanatory

How to use your A-Z and #'s Charts with the Guidance Sheets

Once you've established whom you are speaking with from "Your Team"; using a "yes" or "no" query, ask in what way they like to communicate with you, for instance:

Would you like to use the Guidance Sheets & Chart to communicate with me? "yes or no" please or Would you like to use the Pendulum chart & spell out what you would like to communicate to me? "yes or no" please. **IMPORTANT NOTE**: *It is suggested to get comfortable with the use of the Guidance Sheets first before moving onto direct spelling of words and sentences on the Pendulum chart. Here is how:*

• When using the chart and guidance sheets: Choose the guidance sheet that you would like to get your reading from today; say out loud "I'm using *** guidance sheet." then hold your pendulum above the center mark of your chart and say: "I am ready to begin; Is there a message for me? "yes or no" If the answer is yes then say "I am ready to receive a message" Ask "Your Team" to scan the chart and choose the letter for your message. The pendulum will begin to swing and scan the chart; when it swings repeatedly over one letter, that is the chosen letter. Then you would refer to the letter on the sheet and receive the guidance or message that is written there (similar to Angel or Oracle card messages). If the answer is "no" then it may mean the particular guidance sheet you chose for your message may not be the one your message is on, so go to the next guidance sheet until you get a yes.

Or, by only using your pendulum and the chart you can start asking your own questions and have the answers spelled out to you. Remember to be specific when you ask your questions, so that you receive the most accurate, loving and clear answers possible.

Using the A to Z side of the chart

You can receive direct communication thru spelling of words. Repeat the same steps: Hold your pendulum above the center mark and say: "I am ready to begin" the pendulum will begin to swing and scan the chart; when it swings repeatedly over one letter then that is the chosen letter. Say the letter out loud, then the pendulum will start to scan to the next letter and so on. Keep repeating the same steps until you have received your message. It is a good idea to have a pen and paper handy so you can write down the words you receive. It's okay to stop the process to write down the letters you are receiving and then continue by placing your pendulum over the center mark again. You can also receive general messages about time; spring, summer, fall or winter on this chart.

Please note: You can use your own words that resonate for you when using the chart and communicating; this is what has worked for me when I have used this chart. You can receive as little as one word answers to as much as full sentences. If your pendulum hangs straight down and will not move when you ask a question it either means that your question was not clear enough or that the question you asked was about something that is not for you to know an answer to at this time. **When closing off your session always show Gratitude and say "Thank You"**

Side Note: This is a great way to practice your listening skills. While your pendulum is scanning the chart are you hearing a word come thru that starts with the letter your pendulum is swinging over? Acknowledge the letter that your pendulum is swinging over and then it will move onto the next letter of the word. While you are receiving the start of the word, you may have heard the word come thru before it has been fully spelled out for you. At that time, ask if that is the word it is about to spell out, if you get a "yes" then say "thank you please continue to the next word". If it is "no" then say "thank you, please continue on". Practicing this listening skill brings you closer to trusting the loving guidance you receive on your own so that eventually you will no longer have the need for visual tools like this.

Using the "Numbers" side of the chart

You can also receive messages about time; spring, summer, fall, winter and dates by switching to the numbers chart – you will see the seasons marked on the outer edge of the chart, both on the A to Z Chart and Numbers Chart. If you would like general time; ask your question and your pendulum will start to scan and then repeatedly swing over the season. If you want a specific day it will scan over 1-31 and then repeatedly swing over the chosen date. If you want a month it will scan and go over 1-12 and then repeatedly swing over the chosen month. If you are looking for a specific year it will scan and go over the entire chart and for example if the year is 2021 it will repeatedly swing over the 20 then start scanning again and repeatedly swing over the 21. If you want a complete date, ask it to show you the day first then the month then the year. Please remember that dates are approximate, so leave room for change.

When closing off your session always show Gratitude and say "Thank You"

There are many amazing and unique uses of this communication package. It was designed and infused with the power of "Love and Light". Play, enjoy and have fun connecting with your Higher Self, Angelic team, Guides and the Spirit of Loved Ones, also known throughout is book as "Your Team"

When closing off your session always show Gratitude and say "Thank You"

While using this package, please remember that all guidance you receive is not set in stone, it is a "probable" which means that there is a possibility of change. For example, a circumstance or situation that crosses your path may change or postpone the outcome of the guidance or the information that you had received. Also, that we are all born with "Free Will" which means: regardless of the guidance or information you may receive, you are still the one who decides if you choose to move forward with it or not. It's always "Your Choice" "Your Decision" the guidance you receive is exactly that, it is "Guidance".

BONUS

Create Your Own Guidance Sheets:

In the back of this book you will find blank A-Z Guidance Sheets. This is where you can become creative. These pages are for you to create your own guidance sheets such as: listing more Spirit Animals or Power Animals and discovering which one is yours if it is not already listed in this book. Or if you feel that there is more information that you would like to add to a guidance sheet that is not listed already, feel free to be creative. Use your new Guidance Sheets alongside the Charts & Shielding Intention provided in this book.

NO PEEKING FOLDABLES:

In the back of this book you will find a page with various words or sentences. Each word or sentence will be outlined with a box. This page is to be cut out of the book. This is another unique way to receive messages through your pendulum. Cut the page out of the book, then cut along the lines around each box. Once you have all your slips of paper, fold each slip once and then again so that it is folded twice, be certain that you cannot see the word (almost like a draw slip you would put in a raffle barrel). After they have all been folded, put all your slips in your hand or place in a bowl and make sure they are all mixed up and then drop them on the table. Set your Sacred Space and establish with "Your Team" "Please show me with a "Yes" which slip I should read and "No" to which slip I should not read at this time" then hold your pendulum over the slips and ask your question or ask "what is my message for today" (use whatever wording resonates with you). As you move your pendulum over the slips it should start scanning the folded slips and show you a "yes" to look or a "no" to move on. This is a great way to practice your listening skills. While your pendulum is scanning the slips are you hearing any words come thru? Test yourself and see if what you're hearing is similar to what is chosen with the pendulum on the slip of paper. Keep it light and have fun with it. **Once your reading is over, show gratitude, say thank you for the message to close off your reading**.

Using Angel/Oracle Deck & Your Pendulum

Another way to receive your daily guidance is by using your pendulum along side Angel/Oracle cards. Set your Sacred Space then shuffle your deck, place it on the table and cut the cards into 3 piles. Choose one pile with your pendulum (yes or no) and put the other two off to the side. Spread the cards out onto the table face down so that you cannot see the messages on any of the cards. Once they are spread out, hold your pendulum over the cards. Announce that you are using "***** Deck" (state the name of the deck you are using to "Your Team") Ask "Your Team" to show you "Yes" over the card(s) you should flip to receive your message and show "No" over the cards not to flip. Hold your pendulum over the cards, then slowly move your pendulum over the cards on the table. Your pendulum will start to scan and then move back and forth over each card in the "NO" direction until it locates the card for you to flip over and then it will start to swing in the "YES" direction. Your team will guide you to how many cards are needed for you to receive your message. If you only get one "Yes" to flip a card, then that would represent that you only needed the message on that card. If you get a "Yes" for three cards, then you needed the message from all three cards and so on. Keep it light and enjoy. **Once your reading is over, show gratitude, say thank you for the message to close off your reading**.

Disclaimer:

Please remember that we are human and have free will – this package is to be used with the up most respect towards the other realm. It is meant to help those connect to a realm of beautiful energies with positive intentions and receive positive communication and guidance. This book with all of its components is exactly that: a communication and guidance tool and the information that you receive can change; nothing is set in stone; you have the power to choose.

Under no circumstance is this package to be misused. No responsibility will be assumed for the misuse of this package. There are no guarantees that the "You and Your Pendulum" Package is right for you or will work for you.

For Entertainment Purposes Only. This package is not to replace any legal, financial or healthcare professional advice.

Let's Get The Connection Started

Our Bridge

Our Connection

Our Awakening

SELF- CHECK - DAILY GUIDANCE

A) It's time to make that choice – is there a decision or something weighing heavy on your mind?

B) You did the right thing.

C) You're on the right track.

D) You are on your path.

E) You are in your own way; Get out of the way and allow your angels/guides to help you.

F) Let go of self-doubt; It serves you no purpose.

G) There is a move / change for the better happening soon.

H) Now is not the time – Be patient, you shouldn't make hasty decisions. Take a step back and look at the bigger picture.

I) Journal your ideas; This will start the process in making it a reality.

J) Pay attention to your dreams; Start a dream journal; Watch for similarities and notice the underlying message.

K) There is always a choice; Choose what feels right to you.

L) It is time to live in the now; Stop living in the past; Use the past as lessons learned and experiences to help you live in the now.

M) Listen to your inner guidance; Stop second guessing yourself.

N) Time for a health check; A change in your lifestyle is necessary for optimal health.

O) Opportunities await; Pay attention to the signs & symbols that cross your path.

P) What do you truly desire? Your desires are within reach; Keep your thoughts positive and anything is possible.

Q) Give your Angels and Guides permission to help you; release your worries/fears/burdens to them.

R) Trust in your Angels and Guides they are here to help you;

S) Write down your goals (intentions), what is it that you really want out of your life (big or small); then with positive and true intentions say them every day out loud to your Angelic Team. Notice the positive changes starting to happen for you. You will start checking things off on your list and start adding new things as you go along.

T) Forgiveness is key; It is time to forgive yourself and others; It's time to let go and move forward.

U) Trust your inner guidance; It holds the key.

V) STOP! You are way too hard on yourself.

W) It's okay to stand by what you believe to be true.

X) It's okay to ask for help from others.

Y) Chin Up! Stay positive and keep pushing forward.

Z) Take a deep breath and smile; you are amazing inside and out!

Sheet 1

HEALING MESSAGES - DAILY GUIDANCE

A)   You are loved and supported.

B)   Don't be so hard on yourself.

C)   You are a beautiful soul.

D)   Ask for help – It's okay to ask for help from others & "Your Team"

E)   Surrender and release your worries, fears, burdens to your Angels.

F)   Let your Angels help you in this situation.

G)   Forgiveness is the key to moving forward.

H)   Get more rest.

I)   Time to take better care of yourself.

J)   It's time to live in the NOW! Let go of past situations that no longer serve you any purpose. This is what is holding you back.

K)   Every moment of worry takes away that moment of happiness. So stop worrying so much.

L)   Loved ones in heaven are watching over you, take notice of the Signs & Symbols.

M)   You are protected.

N)   Release the guilt, you have nothing to feel guilty about.

O)   Acceptance will bring you closer to peace.

P)   You need more fun / playtime / laughter.

Q)   Stay strong, you will get thru this situation.

R)   You may not understand it now, but everything happens for a reason.

S)   It's time for positive change.

T)   Keep your thoughts positive! For every negative thought that you may have, think of five positive things that you are blessed with today.

U)   To manifest positive results; keep your intentions and thoughts on a positive path (positive out - positive in)

V)   Divine Timing is key. Be patient.

W)   Meditation is a beautiful way to relax your mind, body & heal your soul.

X)   Pay attention to your visions & dreams; there are profound messages waiting there for you to uncover.

Y)   Allow Balance in your life; As much as you give, it's time to allow yourself to receive from your Physical World and from the Angelic Realm.

Z)   It's the dawn of a new day. Take a deep breath and SMILE!

Sheet 2

LIFE PURPOSE / CAREER - DAILY GUIDANCE

A) New Age Healer

B) Intuitive

C) Health & Fitness

D) Working with animals

E) Counselling / Life Coach

F) Healer—Physiotherapy / Massage / Reflexology...

G) Corporate Office

H) Trades

I) Service Industry

J) Media Arts / Creativity / Music

K) Travel Industry

L) Oracle Cards

M) Writer / Journal

N) Public Speaker

O) Leadership role

P) Volunteer

Q) Culinary Arts

R) Manufacturing Industry

S) Fishing Industry

T) Forestry

U) Environmental

V) Teaching / Instructing

W) Entrepreneur

X) Legal

Y) Healthcare

Z) Armed Forces

MESSAGES FROM YOUR ANGELIC TEAM - DAILY GUIDANCE

A) Abundance & Prosperity are within reach. Keep your thoughts positive.

B) You are on your path.

C) Give it more thought – Now is not the time to make hasty decisions. Look at the situation with a different perspective.

D) That's a good idea.

E) You will be okay.

F) Let go of any doubt. You are doing the right thing.

G) Seek other options.

H) Stay humble. Always show gratitude where gratitude is due.

I) Circumstances can change the outcome.

J) Not the right time.

K) Keep your heart and mind open.

L) This situation is not right for you.

M) Your guides are trying to communicate with you. Watch for signs.

N) Take better care of yourself. Get more rest and exercise.

O) It's time to take a step back and review the situation.

P) Take back your power.

Q) Keep your thoughts, intentions and goals positive and watch the doors open for you. It's your time to shine.

R) Pay attention to your dreams and ideas. Keep a journal

S) This is your Soul's journey, things are as they should be at this moment in time, just breathe.

T) You are loved and supported.

U) Trust your feelings – A shift/positive changes are on the horizon.

V) You know your next move. It's time to take that next step.

W) No need to worry.

X) Pay attention to the signs. You are being guided.

Y) Your Angelic Team is waiting for permission to help you—Just ask!

Z) It's time to take that next step.

Sheet 4

ROMANCE / LOVE - DAILY GUIDANCE

A) Soulmate.

B) Life partner.

C) He / She Loves You.

D) Be patient, there is no need to worry.

E) The right person will come along.

F) You will know. Trust your intuition.

G) You are worthy of love.

H) You are connected thru past life events.

I) Let go of the past.

J) Make the effort.

K) Don't be afraid.

L) Everything is happening as it should.

M) Separation.

N) Worth the wait.

O) He / She is not the one.

P) You will have your answer very soon.

Q) Walk away.

R) Marriage / Union.

S) Children are part of the factor.

T) New Beginning.

U) True Love.

V) Need to talk about it – Take the time to sit down and discuss what is bothering you.

W) Deception / Troubles.

X) Reconciliation

Y) Stay positive, your prayers are being answered.

Z) It's okay to move forward.

TALKING TO LOVED ONES – DAILY GUIDANCE

A)   I never left you; I just had to go.

B)   You have nothing to feel guilty for.

C)   I didn't want you to remember me that way.

D)   I'm just a thought away.

E)   Want you to live. Live in the now and enjoy the moments.

F)   It's okay for you to move forward.

G)   I want you to be happy again.

H)   Thank you for being my rock.

I)   I am with you; take notice of the signs.

J)   There is no such thing as good-bye.

K)   Journal your dreams; There is a message there for you.

L)   We will see each other again.

M)   Stay strong; Other people need you also.

N)   There is no time limit on grief; But it will get easier.

O)   Let go of what no longer serves you any purpose.

P)   You don't need to hang on so tight; I am always around.

Q)   This was my exit point; I learned my life lessons.

R)   You may not understand now; But everything happens for a reason.

S)   You don't have to worry about me; I am happy and safe.

T)   I love you.

U)   I'm not alone here; I am very loved.

V)   What you see, feel, sense, and know is true; TRUST

W)   There is no such thing as death; it is only another state of being.

X)   You have guides, guardian angels and loved ones always around you.

Y)   You are safe.

Z)   I know how much you miss me; But it was my time to go and there was no way that you could have changed things; Please understand and there is no need to feel guilty.

Sheet 6

COMMUNICATING WITH YOUR FURRY FRIENDS (Living Pets)
DAILY GUIDANCE

1) I am here for you.
2) I need a change in my diet. I am bored with my food.
3) I don't feel well.
4) I want to be outside more.
5) I won't runaway.
6) You're my mom/dad now.
7) I need more exercise.
8) I am happy.
9) I am sad sometimes.
10) I love you.
11) I count on you.
12) I love playtime.
13) My head hurts.
14) Don't be sad.
15) You will be okay.
16) My teeth hurt.
17) I feel stressed sometimes.
18) My stomach hurts.
19) feel everything you feel.
20) I am healthy.
21) I worry about you sometimes.
22) I see the Angels.
23) I see those who belong with you in Spirit.
24) I miss him/her too.
25) I love cuddles.
26) I know what you are thinking and I understand what you say to me.
27) I like to have conversations with you.
28) They have a message for you.
29) I don't like strangers.
30) I don't like the vet.
31) I miss you when you are away and I am happy when you come home..

Sheet 7

WHO ARE MY SPIRIT ANIMAL GUIDES
WHO IS MY POWER ANIMAL

A)	BEAR	**1)**	LEMUR
B)	WOLF	**2)**	FOX
C)	HORSE	**3)**	WEASEL
D)	EAGLE	**4)**	WOLVERINE
E)	DOG	**5)**	WALRUS
F)	CAT	**6)**	DOLPHIN
G)	LION	**7)**	MOLE
H)	ORCA	**8)**	LIZARD
I)	SNAKE	**9)**	HYENA
J)	HAWK	**10)**	IBIS
K)	ELEPHANT	**11)**	HUMMINGBIRD
L)	OWL	**12)**	HARE / RABBIT
M)	DEER	**13)**	GROUNDHOG
N)	BADGER	**14)**	MOUNTAIN GOAT
O)	COYOTE	**15)**	ANTELOPE
P)	COUGAR	**16)**	BABOON
Q)	RAVEN	**17)**	ARMADILLO
R)	LYNX/BOBCAT	**18)**	BAT
S)	ALLIGATOR	**19)**	BEE
T)	BEAVER	**20)**	BLUE JAY
U)	TIGER	**21)**	BUFFALO
V)	TURTLE	**22)**	BULL
W)	SWAN	**23)**	BUTTERFLY
X)	PHOENIX	**24)**	CHEETAH
Y)	UNICORN	**25)**	CHIMPANZEE
Z)	SPIDER	**26)**	CONDOR
		27)	DOVE
		28)	DRAGONFLY
		29)	DRAGON
		30)	FALCON
		31)	GORILLA

Sheet 8

NOTES :

_____
_____
_____
_____
_____
_____
_____
_____
_____
_____
_____
_____
_____
_____
_____
_____
_____
_____
_____
_____
_____
_____
_____
_____

Create Your Own Guidance Sheet

TITLE:

A. _____

B. _____

C. _____

D. _____

E. _____

F. _____

G. _____

H. _____

I. _____

J. _____

K. _____

L. _____

M. _____

N. _____

O. _____

P. _____

Q. _____

R. _____

S. _____

T. _____

U. _____

V. _____

W. _____

X. _____

Y. _____

Z. _____

Create Your Own Guidance Sheet

TITLE: _____

A. _____

B. _____

C. _____

D. _____

E. _____

F. _____

G. _____

H. _____

I. _____

J. _____

K. _____

L. _____

M. _____

N. _____

O. _____

P. _____

Q. _____

R. _____

S. _____

T. _____

U. _____

V. _____

W. _____

X. _____

Y. _____

Z. _____

Create Your Own Guidance Sheet

TITLE:

A. _____

B. _____

C. _____

D. _____

E. _____

F. _____

G. _____

H. _____

I. _____

J. _____

K. _____

L. _____

M. _____

N. _____

O. _____

P. _____

Q. _____

R. _____

S. _____

T. _____

U. _____

V. _____

W. _____

X. _____

Y. _____

Z. _____

Our Bridge

Our Connection

Our Awakening

NO PEEKING FOLDABLES

YES	*NO*	*YOU ARE ON THE RIGHT TRACK*	*IT'S OKAY FOR YOU TO ASK FOR HELP*
YOU'RE EXACTLY WHERE YOU NEED TO BE AT THIS MOMENT	*WAIT*	*I / WE LOVE YOU*	*IT'S TIME TO MOVE FORWARD*
PAY ATTENTION TO YOUR DREAMS – THERE IS A MESSAGE WAITING	*LET GO OF WHAT NO LONGER SERVES YOU ANY PURPOSE*	*LIVE IN THE "NOW" IT'S TIME FOR YOU TO ENJOY THE MOMENTS*	*WHAT YOU FEEL, SEE, SENSE & KNOW IS TRUE "TRUST"*
STAY STRONG OTHER PEOPLE NEED YOU ALSO	*BEFORE YOU DECIDE TAKE A STEP BACK AND LOOK AT THE BIGGER PICTURE*	*BE PATIENT THERE IS NO NEED TO WORRY*	*TAKE NOTICE OF THE SIGNS & SYMBOLS YOU ARE BEING GUIDED*

CREATE YOUR OWN
"NO PEEKING FOLDABLES"

Our Bridge

Our Connection

Our Awakening

YOU AND YOUR PENDULUM

A Diagonal Swing Towards The Right Would Represent
You Are Going To Be Ok / Everything is ok

You're doing great

I am ok / I am doing great

Clockwise Would Represent Yes
Swing Back & Forth / North-South Represents No

You Have The Right Idea

Yes

On the right path

On the right track

Yes

Yes

NO

On the right track

On the right path

You Have The Right Idea

THANK YOU / YOU ARE WELCOME

A Diagonal Swing Towards The Left Would Represent
I Love you / We love you

Counter Clockwise Could Reference The Following:
You are on the right path
You are on the right track
You have the right idea

Setting Your Sacred Space (Shielding Thoughts & Intentions)

Archangel Michael, All Divine, All Of Which Who Belong With Me and Who Are Of 100% Pure White Light.

Please Shield Me To Prevent My Ego, Willful and Wishful Thinking And My Thoughts From Influencing Any Messages That I May Receive On My Pendulum.
Please Also Shield The Thoughts Of Others and Keep Them From Influencing The Messages That I Receive On My Pendulum.
Only Beings Of 100% Pure White Light, The Divine And Those Who Belong With Me Be Allowed To Communicate Loving, Truthful and Honest Messages Which Serve Me For My Highest
Purpose And Which Are Only For My Best Interest. I am aware that the guidance I receive is for the "NOW" And The Messages I Receive Are The Messages I Will Accept.
With Grace And Gratitude I Ask That I Am Always Shielded and Safe In Your White Light Of Protection Forever and Always . So It Is, So It Is Set, So It Will Be.

You and Your Pendulum

Winter

Fall

Fall

Winter

On the right path

Yes

On the right track

Yes

Yes

On the right track

Yes

On the right path

NO

Spring

Summer

Summer

Spring

THANK YOU / YOU ARE WELCOME

Setting Your Sacred Space (Shielding Thoughts & Intentions)

Archangel Michael, All Divine, All Of Which Who Belong With Me And Who Are Of 100% Pure White Light.

Please Shield Me To Prevent My Ego, Willful and Wishful Thinking And My Thoughts From Influencing Any Messages That I May Receive On My Pendulum.
Please Also Shield The Thoughts Of Others and Keep Them From Influencing The Messages That I Receive On My Pendulum.

Only Beings Of 100% Pure White Light, The Divine And Those Who Belong With Me Be Allowed To Communicate Loving, Truthful and Honest Messages
Which Serve Me For My Highest Purpose And Which Are Only For My Best Interest. I Am Aware That The Guidance I Receive Is For The "NOW" And The
Messages I Receive Are The Messages I Will Accept. With Grace And Gratitude I Ask That I Am Always Shielded and Safe In Your White Light Of Protection
Forever and Always . So It Is, So It Is Set, So It Will Be.

Copyright 2020 Carol Calmes

You and Your Pendulum

Winter

Fall

Winter

Fall

On the right path

Yes

On the right track

Yes

Yes

On the right path

NO

Yes

On the right track

Summer

Spring

Summer

Spring

THANK YOU / YOU ARE WELCOME

Setting Your Sacred Space (Shielding Thoughts & Intentions)

Archangel Michael, All Divine, All Of Which Who Belong With Me And Who Are Of 100% Pure White Light.
Please Shield Me To Prevent My Ego, Willful and Wishful Thinking And My Thoughts From Influencing Any Messages That I May Receive On My Pendulum.
Please Also Shield The Thoughts Of Others and Keep Them From Influencing The Messages That I Receive On My Pendulum.
Only Beings Of 100% Pure White Light, The Divine And Those Who Belong With Me Be Allowed To Communicate Loving, Truthful and Honest Messages
Which Serve Me For My Highest Purpose And Which Are Only For My Best Interest. I Am Aware That The Guidance I Receive Is For The "NOW" And The
Messages I Receive Are The Messages I Will Accept. With Grace And Gratitude I Ask That I Am Always Shielded and Safe In Your White Light Of Protection
Forever and Always . So It Is, So It Is Set, So It Will Be.

Printed in the United States
By Bookmasters